The View from the Porch

"LIKING YOURSELF WON'T SOLVE ANYTHING." - PUP

J. GRESHAM

Copyright © 2011 J. Gresham
All rights reserved.

ISBN:0-615-35347-9
ISBN-13:978-0-615-35347-0
LCCN:2010902423

I would like to thank the following people who supported and encouraged this project: Michele Ives, Sián White, Mary Baird, Becky & Dave Moffett-Moore, Dan Schupert, Vera Tiani and Lindsey VanBelleghem

Human pride is not worth while; there is always something lying in wait to take the wind out of it.

-Mark Twain

Preface

My dog Jack can talk. I won't waste time trying to convince you that it's true, but I do want to share the conversations that began late last winter on our back porch. You can read them and make up your own mind. The conversations were helpful to me and they might be helpful to you, even if you don't believe it. Anyway, he deserves all of the credit for this, so I'm typing his version of the story. Here it is.

-Leo

Introduction

Everything in this book seems so simple and obvious that I can't believe it had to be written, but I'm a dog, and what is obvious to me isn't necessarily obvious to humans. Not even smart humans like my friend Leo. As smart as he is, even Leo struggled to accept ideas that are, to a dog, pretty basic. You probably would have struggled too, had we not written this book for you.

Writing it was Leo's idea. When he first suggested it, I was apprehensive. I tried to tell him that this is not a story filled with the kind of drama that humans seem to like. It has some of the right components: a nice guy who's worth cheering for, and a hard-earned epiphany. But the change in his life was relatively subtle. He's not a drug addict who got clean. He's not a homeless man who rebuilt his life and climbed the corporate ladder. This is a story about a guy who learns a few helpful things from his dog. It's probably not even the first story about that, so I was resistant. But Leo continued to push. He said, "Some of the smartest people, the people who are the most confident that they have things figured out, are still missing something, something dogs have always known. And if reading our story helps them figure it out, they'll appreciate it."

I said, "Humans don't want to be told they're missing something. I know humans, they don't take that kind of thing well. They'll be defensive."

"Well, yeah, that might be true. But it's usually other humans that make them defensive," he said. "Perhaps they'll be more receptive if they hear it from a dog."

"You were smart enough to listen to a dog, but other humans might not be so wise," I said.

"It wasn't about being smart. It was about being receptive. I think there is something about dogs that just makes people a little more receptive. They put their defenses down a bit."

He was right. We can be very cute. People respond well to cute, so I agreed to help create the book. At least I might save a few dogs the trouble of having to explain this stuff to their humans.

After he convinced me to help create the book, there was still the problem of figuring out how we would tell our story. We could have simply summarized the key messages that I shared with Leo, and wrapped it up in an organized-by-topic self-help book. We decided against that. Rather than telling you what he discovered, we decided that we should let you listen in on the conversations that helped him discover it.

I trust in your ability to translate these conversations into your own circumstances, but I will occasionally offer some introductory thoughts to help explain how they might apply to other people. And maybe you don't even need such a thing. In that case, congratulations for being nearly as smart as a dog.

I would have been content to let our conversations tell the story, but Leo insisted that people like to have details about the characters and settings in the stories they read. Fine. I'll say a little about Leo. He's forty-something. The dark floppy hair he had when I met him is on its way to gray. When he pushes it back under a baseball cap his look changes from hippy guy to sporty guy. His job at a landscape and garden company puts him outside a lot. He owes his fit body and tan face to it. His girlfriend Liz is probably the only person he'll dress up for, and they are a sharp couple when he does.

It's worth mentioning that Leo is pretty intelligent for a human. A dog isn't going to waste his time talking to just any dumb human. But he is not a genius; he was just smart enough to be receptive when he needed to be. His curiosity was also helpful. He likes to learn. He reads philosophy, religion, science and an assortment of popular novels. Also, he likes to surround himself with nature. The porch where we wrote most of this story looks out over a park, and we walk there often. I tend to get along better with humans who enjoy nature. They're curious about other life forms and I think it's a reflection of their openness to other perspectives. If you have some of these traits in common with Leo, this story might be for you.

Each time Leo finished one of those philosophy or psychology books, he would go out into the world feeling as if he had finally acquired the last piece of some mental puzzle, some new trick that would allow him to have the feeling that he wanted. But last winter when he returned from work with news of a promotion it became clear that, even with that trick, he hadn't acquired a canine level of wisdom. That night I knew I wouldn't be able to stay quiet and give his fuzzy human logic a chance to ruin us. So, when he asked for it, I offered some help. Some might say that what he learned from me is just another one of those tricks. Maybe, but I bet you know some dogs that are happier than you have ever been, so perhaps it will be worth an hour or two in your comfortable chair, reading this book

Chapter 1

The first winter day that cardinals sang

To be a rescued stray is lucky enough, but to be rescued by a guy like Leo is even luckier. He's even-tempered and compassionate. He's a hard worker, but always makes time to sit and relax with me. His appreciation of the outdoors means that I get to be outdoors a lot too. We had a big, wild yard at the edge of a park with trails through forests and fields. We walked those trails as often as we could. I lived with Leo for three years before I ever had a single worry. That worry came one February evening when Leo returned from work.

The View from the Porch

It had been the kind of February day that is just sunny and melty enough to remind you that winter doesn't last forever. Cardinals sang to the rest of the birds that they are brave enough to begin their courtship, even if we had a few more winter storms left before spring. The winter cold, which locks up the sounds and scents of nature, had loosened its grip just slightly. My nose had much to sort through on our walk that day. My ears pulled my attention to dozens of scurrying and singing animals, but Leo seemed oblivious to the signs that the cold, slushy winter was on its way out. He had that look he gets when he has something interesting to say, but he was silent for the duration of our walk. His face was on the verge of a smile but it never fully developed. It was something he wanted to be happy about, but wasn't yet.

After dinner, when we were settled on the porch, it didn't take long for him to come out with it.

"I think they might offer me a promotion."

The smile finally developed on his face. I got up from my rug and put my paw on his thigh. "Thanks, Pup," he said, rubbing my ears. He tells people that my name is Jack, but he always calls me Pup.

He took a deep breath and said, "They've been talking about opening a new store in Granger."

I didn't know where Granger was, but the smile left his face when he said it.

"I'd be getting a pretty good raise. Maybe I could even think about getting a new home. I might have to, actually. It would be a long drive to Granger from here."

"What about the park!?" I nearly blurted out, but stopped myself just in time. I had never spoken to Leo. Our friendship had never required it. Most friendships between a human and a dog work fine without the incessant talking that humans inflict on each other. Dogs know that they can get most of what they want with nonverbal communication. They also know that if they were ever foolish enough to speak to their human friends, they'd end up having to explain all kinds of things.

Leo continued to make a case for his promotion. "Yeah, maybe if I found a nice house, I'd surprise Liz. I could take her there to tell her the good news. And ask her to marry me."

I tried to remain calm, but I could see this going badly. That was the first evening I seriously contemplated talking to Leo. It seemed quite likely that he would need my help with this.

The View from the Porch

I dropped my head onto his thigh. He rubbed my ears again. He seemed to be trying to comfort me. *He has already decided to accept the promotion,* I thought.

I didn't want to discourage him, but I tend to be suspicious of highly motivated humans. Motivation is not in itself a bad thing, but often humans don't thoroughly consider what they really hope to gain. They dress it up with phrases like "reaching my potential" but usually it's about something else. I wanted to ask him, "How will your days *feel* when you run that store? What will be better after you reach this goal?"

Perhaps he thought that his days would feel better if he had a little more income. He might get a place with a pond or a bigger garden or a fenced-in yard. He might eat better. Or take a more luxurious vacation with Liz. These could have been his motivators and they are fine, so I said nothing. I slept uneasily that night.

* * *

Chapter 2

The day that Leo brought me a pig's ear

He came home from work a few minutes later than usual. He arrived with a pig's ear which he set on the counter. I could smell it there, but he waited until after dinner and a short walk to give it to me on the back porch. It was hickory smoked. He sat down with his tea as I began gnawing on the salty chew. I was just starting to get it softened and dripping with hickory flavor when Leo said, "Well, Pup, they offered me that position."

Damn, I had almost forgotten about it.

The View from the Porch

"Yep, they bought the property, they're starting some renovations soon, and in a few months, I'll be the manager... *if* I decide to accept." He sipped his tea. "I think I will. I have some time to think about it though." He sipped his tea again. I said nothing.

"I think it will be a good thing for both of us, Pup."

I wanted to know *how*. How will it be a good thing? If he would have just told me, right then, how he thought it would make our lives better, I never would have had to speak to him. But he didn't, and I was sure that it was because he wasn't really thinking about it like that. Instead he was thinking about it like a human. So I couldn't let him do it. I decided right then, that I would come up with a plan to counsel my best friend.

Up to that point in our friendship I had apparently chosen to ignore any sign that Leo was unhappy with his life. It was an easy mistake. He was happier than most people. At work he found some fulfillment in his ability to use his body and mind to create attractive landscapes. At home he found solitude and nature in his backyard and in the park beyond. His relationship with Liz seemed healthy, and provided him with a partner for weekend adventures, be they on rivers, lakes, trails, or in downtown restaurants.

Sometimes, though, humans arrive at the right thing by accident. The more he talked about the promotion the more I felt as if Leo had created our peaceful life with luck rather than wisdom. Perhaps I could have just told him that, right there on the porch that evening. But if indeed it was luck, I would have to plan carefully to provide him with the wisdom to make sure that his promotion didn't mess up our lives.

I began thinking about how to start a conversation that could show him what he needed to see. That night I tried to plan it all out. Instead of resting comfortably on my rug I found myself rehearsing the conversation. But the more I thought about it, the more I realized I was thinking like a human. When I decided our conversation would go where it needed to go, sleep came easily. An hour later, I awoke to the sound of Leo's spoon rattling in his empty tea cup as he gathered his stuff from the end table and called me to bed.

* * *

Chapter 3

The day that the hawk killed something below the grapevine tangle

Sometimes Leo comes home from work and tells me about some insect or bird or flower that he saw. I like to listen to him talk about nature. Sometimes he comes home and tells me about people, but I always like it more when he tells me about nature. The first day I talked to Leo was a day on which he shared an interesting story about a hawk.

When he returned from work that day, we took our daily walk in the park. The sky was gray, and a fresh layer

The View from the Porch

of snow had smoothed the landscape. There were no other human tracks on the trail. It was a day that a human might call barren, though my nose told me that the park was still very much alive. Leo is not usually inclined to let such a day bring him down, but he was unusually quiet while we walked, and I could tell there were a lot of words in his head.

After dinner, he made tea and we sat on the back porch. He was silent for a while, then finally said, "I saw something today that I've never seen before."

I looked up from my spot on the rug. "This sounds like it will be a nature story," I thought.

"This morning I was shoveling snow behind the greenhouse when a reflection in the glass caught my eye. Something large flew by, behind me. I turned just in time to see a Cooper's hawk pull up and land in a pine at the edge of the woods. I've seen Cooper's hawks before. I've seen their speed and maneuverability, but today I saw something different.

"It took me a while to realize what was so different. It was the take-off. Apparently I had never seen one take-off from its perch. Usually, when I see a Cooper's hawk hunting, it's zooming in, trying to surprise its prey. They'll spot a smaller bird from a distance, then fly low and fast, using a bush or a tree or a house to hide their approach until the last second." He pointed out to the yard where we had seen this happen before, then his hand glided through the air mimicking the hawk. "Then they swing around the corner and close the distance before the prey can react. If its target, or any other birds, sees the hawk coming, one sends out an alarm and they all scatter into bushes, or freeze like statues hoping it won't see them. Sometimes the hawk will keep trying. I've seen them plunge into the brush to flush out a bird. But, most of the time, when there is good cover for the songbirds, the hawk will usually leave and go try some other area.

"Today, this hawk saw a target in the pine, but the other birds saw him coming and whistled a warning. He lost the element of surprise. And he couldn't flush anybody from their hiding spots. So the hawk waited in the pine where I saw him land. I watched him for a while, as he looked around hoping to catch someone gliding into the scene unaware. I have to admit, I was hoping he'd catch something. Even though I fill the birdfeeders every morning, and like watching the birds that visit back there, I know this hawk is part of the system too. And there's something about seeing a predator in action that really makes you feel as if the mechanisms of nature still work.

"I was about to get back to shoveling, when I saw his head turn, just slightly, toward the forest. Then I saw the

The View from the Porch

take-off. I have seen the kill before...on TV, and in real life a few times, back here in the yard. But I can't remember ever seeing a take-off. This bird instantly changed from a still thing to a missile. From a feathery fluff trying to stay warm on a branch, to a bullet. There was just a little turn of the head before this explosion of energy. Then it moved through the forest, a real dense part of the forest, in an unbelievably straight line, somehow avoiding all the trees and shrubs and vines. I lost sight of it as it dropped low behind a grapevine tangle. I didn't see the kill this time. But the take-off...man, it was amazing."

He paused and sipped his tea. He sat silently for a moment.

"It seemed extraordinary, but in the animal world, I guess it was just a simple, well-tuned, mechanical act of survival. The hawk is not concerned with extraordinary. It was only concerned with the meal below the grapevine tangle."

Keep going Leo, I thought.

"On a cold, March day, I shouldn't envy a bird whose survival depends on the precision of its every movement, but how liberating it must be to aim oneself at comfort, live with that singular purpose, and never get tied up in quests to be extraordinary. You seem to do it."

J. Gresham

Of course.

"What's the secret, Jack? Is it just your simple brain? Or is it an enlightened brain? Are you and the hawk enlightened beings, while we humans are helpless?"

I looked up without lifting my head off my paws. I wanted him to say a little more, but he stopped there and we went to bed. After an hour of turning and adjusting restlessly, he finally relaxed and was nearly asleep, when an owl hooted in the backyard. Leo must've heard it because he got up and went to the porch to listen. I followed him.

"Was that a dream?" He asked.

I said nothing. He sat on the porch, waiting for his eyes to adjust to the darkness. He scanned the tree line for the silhouette of the owl. Then he asked me again about my strategy.

"You've charmed your way into getting me to give you room and board," he said, as he settled into his chair. "You don't get stressed about work. What's your secret Jack?"

I wiggled my tail in approval of his question. He looked down at me, but his mind seemed far away. I think he was trying to imagine my reality.

The View from the Porch

"It does seem like you enjoy a happier existence. I've read a lot of philosophy and religion, but if dogs could write, I think you'd write the best books yet. You really seem to have mastered the art of living well, and here you are, available for consultation... if only you could speak the words to describe it.

"Maybe that's your secret. No words. How often are our problems really just wrong words in our heads? Sometimes it seems that no words must be better than the wrong words. You know a few words, but I doubt that you are aware of them unless you are about to get some *food*, or go to the *park*. I guess people think that the quantity and complexity of our words makes us superior. It isn't true, is it, Jack? Why do we need so many words?"

I wagged my tail. Leo stared off into the darkness at the edge of the yard.

"Perhaps people who practice meditation get close, because meditation can get their mind into a wordless state, if they practice a lot. I've tried meditation, but it's hard. Words come into your head and your mind goes in every direction. But I like it. I always seem to have a clearer head after I do it."

Then Leo sat silently. He breathed deeply. He was still, except to turn his head toward some sound from the woods.

I could hear that deep hoot from the owl in the park, but I didn't think it was loud enough for Leo to hear. His breathing fell into a steady rhythm. He seemed unburdened by all the words that normally swim in his head. He felt the warmth of his sweater and the cold on his face.

I was warm and comfortable on my rug. I always liked Leo very much, but he had always been a very different kind of animal, until that night. I looked up at him from my rug to see the comfort in his face and body. For once I felt that the differences between us were small. I stood and turned toward him. I put my paw on his thigh. He looked into my eyes and listened for an explanation. And listened. And listened. Then...I said it. I spoke to Leo.

I said, *People mostly use words just to create a unique identity.*

He turned to me with wide eyes. *What surprised him?* I wondered. The fact that I spoke? Or what I said? I didn't know, but thought it was best to let him think about it a while. So I didn't answer him when he asked, "Aren't we already truly unique individuals? Why would we mostly use our words to try to create what already exists?"

Speaking to a human was risky, but it had to be done and I felt fine about it. Dogs know better than to waste energy regretting their actions. Many more conversations would be

The View from the Porch

needed to help Leo make the right decision about his job, but I had reason to be confident in Leo, confident that our conversations would take us where we needed to go. I eased down onto my rug and slept.

* * *

Chapter 4

The day that a shrew tunneled in the snow

Perhaps I could have just tried to convince Leo that living near the park was too great to give up, but that would have been taking the easy way out. I feared that his interest in the promotion was related to an underlying problem that needed to be fixed if we were going to have real peace, wherever we live. Humans have attempted to understand and describe this problem before. They have used words like self-esteem and insecurity. I'd prefer not to attach those words to our conversation because humans have tainted them

The View from the Porch

with some pretty ridiculous ideas. It is fair to say though, that Leo's problem was related to those terms. So our conversation wasn't just about moving. It was about getting him to understand the factors that made him want to move and how those factors affected everything. So if it seems that our discussion had nothing to do with a house, that was the plan. Leo never thought it was about a house either.

The next opportunity to speak came just a few days later. He had attempted to initiate conversations before then, but there is a certain way to introduce humans to these things and I needed to wait for just the right kind of question, the right kind of example to illustrate my point. Laying it all out at once, getting right to the real heart of the matter, would have overwhelmed him. Human beliefs are complex. They are made of so many little parts. Some of those parts were put in place in childhood, and many humans haven't bothered to think about them much as adults. I knew that if our conversation was going to be helpful to Leo, he needed to confront some of his oldest beliefs. His beliefs about bragging were a good example. Children are taught not to brag. Then they grow up and go through adulthood accepting what they learned as children, with nothing but a little talk show pop-psychology advice added to their limited understanding of it. A person brags because he has low self-esteem, right? Maybe, but how quickly people jump to that conclusion and rest there comfortably.

When Leo returned from work that day we went to the porch to see what birds were visiting the feeders. He stood close to the glass where he could see around the bushes in the corner of the yard. A few chickadees and a nuthatch took turns picking sunflower seeds from the tall feeder. Leo arched and twisted his sore back until it cracked. He took a deep breath and turned his neck from side to side and front to back. He suddenly stopped his stretching and stooped low toward the bottom of the window. I join him to see what caught his eye. Leaves and patches of melting snow covered the yard. One little patch near a large stone moved. A small mound of the snow seemed to hop right off the top. Then, from the dirty leaves at the edge of the snow, a shrew appeared. I puffed at it to let Leo know we had a visitor, but I think he already knew. "It's a shrew," he said, wiping the steam from my breath off the glass. He watched for several more minutes as the shrew ran along the ground, revealing a well-worn route between a pile of fallen sunflower seeds and his large stone shelter. "Wow, he's an energetic little guy," he said as he settled down into his chair. I plopped down on the rug at his feet. He jotted a few things in his notebook.

The View from the Porch

He sat quietly until he finished his tea, then told me about something that happened that day that reminded him of our previous conversation.

"When we walk in the park, do the other dogs brag about their accomplishments?" He asked. "I saw this guy Nick today at the gas station. I haven't seen him in a few years so I go over to him to see what he's been up to. He breaks into this list of accomplishments. He just ran his first marathon. Just bought a house in Knollwood. And he just got his masters degree. Great, I am happy for him. But then he says that he scored higher on some test than any other person in the masters program. Why do people feel the need to brag about stuff like that?"

I wagged my tail, happy for the opportunity to continue our conversation.

Did you ask him how he was?

"Well, yeah."

What did you think he would say when you asked him that? What kind of things did you think he would talk about?

"I don't know. Tell me about his kids, tell me about his job, that kind of stuff."

Did he?

"Yeah, but that other stuff seemed unnecessary."

Leo, how does a person choose which details to include in their conversations with other people? It seems complicated.

"Hmm. I guess it depends on the kind of conversation. When you're catching up with an old friend... I guess you tell them about your job... and family."

Things you're proud of?

"Yeah, but... not just because you're proud. Those are the things that take up most of your time and energy."

But it's OK to be proud of it, right?

"Sure. But why does he feel the need to say that he scored higher than anyone else?"

Why do you say 'feel the need'?

"Well...I...I just mean why does he feel compelled to bring that up?"

Does that bit of information stand out as particularly irrelevant compared with all the other absolutely vital things he mentioned?

The View from the Porch

Leo shifted in his chair. He opened his mouth to speak, but apparently didn't have any words ready, so he closed it and thought for a moment.

If you had gone another year without seeing him you would be alright without any of the information he gave you. About his kids, his job— none of it is practical information to you. But I wonder why a person should choose not to tell you about some superior skill they have. Of all the things that a person might include in a story, why not that? If a person you hadn't seen in a while told you the color of their toothbrush, it would be weird, but you probably wouldn't be offended by it. Is the color of their toothbrush more or less meaningful than a superior score on a test? The test score seems like a relatively interesting part of the drama of a life. And isn't that what you usually share when you catch up with old friends? So much of what is intended but unsaid in a conversation seems to be about things you're proud of— why should you vilify someone just because he says it directly?

Leo shifted in his chair again.

You don't want him to tell you that detail because it breaks the silly rules of superiority that you people have invented.

"They're not just silly rules. There are practical reasons for behaving that way."

I waited for his reasons. I wiggled my tail when I knew he realized his reasons were weak. But he wasn't ready to give up on his argument. He answered, "I mean, they're basic rules of decency. What would it be like if we were always going around one-upping each other? Telling each other how great we are? It's just disrespectful."

I suppose if the goal is to make someone feel low, it isn't good. But why are you so sure that was his goal?

"What else would it be though? Even if he is not trying to put someone else down, does he really need to have his accomplishments validated like that?"

You have no idea what he needs. But you sure seem to have those rules mastered.

"What rules are you talking about?"

The bragging rules. The self-esteem rules. All of it...Here are the people rules about all this... tell me if I've got this wrong: When a person says he is inferior, other people should intervene to keep him from feeling inferior. But if a person says that he is superior he has broken the rules. You are supposed to let other people say that. No one is inferior and no one is superior unless, of course, someone else says you are superior as a compliment... probably to make you feel superior... or not inferior... or something. Do I have that about right, Leo?

The View from the Porch

"I suppose."

He sat silently for a while trying to come up with a way around it.

"It just seems like there is still some better way than commenting on your own superiority."

What if Nick doesn't even value superiority that much? What if he spoke about his score because of the practical consequences? Maybe his advisor will include that information in a recommendation for a job. Maybe he is excited about the career opportunities that are now available.

"You didn't see the look on his face. It was all about pride."

Yeah, well, I wasn't there. And certainly there are many people who seem to be driven by pride. If that is Nick's problem, then that is Nick's problem. But I think that your quickness to vilify Nick says something about your own pride.

"My pride? He's the one that was bragging!"

And why is that hurtful to you?

He stammered for an answer. Bragging is just wrong, he wanted to say, but he knew that I would make him explain why.

Do you see how these rules have helped you hide your desire to be superior? I know that you don't need *to be superior to Nick, but you want to be, don't you?*

He sighed, as he tried to bring himself to say "no". He said nothing.

These rules help you believe that Nick is the one doing something wrong.

I paused to let him consider it. He shifted uneasily in his chair. Again he wanted to deny it, but the truth was settling in.

Don't feel bad Leo, there's a reason you got so attached to these rules. There's a reason people think about self-esteem so much. It works in a lot of situations. Sometimes it is important to realize that someone in your life lacks esteem, but other times...many other times...it just keeps you from acknowledging your own quest for superiority. Or your dissatisfaction with your inferiority.

He's a better marathon runner isn't he? There's not much reason to start ranking your marathons skills, but if you were to do that, he's a better runner right? I have never seen you run a marathon. Some combination of your body, your experience, and your marathon-running skills means that Nick is a better marathon runner. So you might say you are inferior to Nick as a marathon runner.

The View from the Porch

That is a fact that doesn't bother you much, because you don't value marathon running. But when someone comes at you with superiority in an area that you value, and perhaps reminds you that you didn't finish college, then you are pretty quick to remember those rules. You call him out and note his inferior knowledge of the superiority rules. Probably because you are motivated by the same pride that you suspect motivated him to say the things in the first place.

"Well, isn't Nick just trying to use words to create a unique identity?"

We don't know what Nick was trying to do. The only thing we know about Nick is that he didn't follow the stupid rules. Maybe that is why he has enjoyed such success. He is not wasting time showing off his humility. Maybe he knows exactly what pop-psychology has to say about people who brag, that they are compensating for their inferiority. And maybe he just doesn't care because he knows that isn't his issue. Maybe he feels real joy about his opportunities.

"But don't you think there really are a lot of people who brag because they actually feel inferior and need validation?"

Of course there are people like that. But I don't think they are really so different than the people who appoint themselves enforcers of the silly superiority rules.

"Like me?"

I said nothing. I curled into a ball on the rug, tucking my head down to my feet. I didn't really have an opinion about what kind of guy Nick was. Leo may have been right. Nick may have been an insecure jerk who flaunts his success to everyone he sees. But that really wasn't the point. Leo needed to see how his own esteem affected his interpretation of other people's behavior. He needed to see that his awareness of the connection between bragging and self-esteem didn't necessarily mean he understood esteem. On that night he was still weeks away from understanding it.

I raised an eyebrow toward Leo to check that he was pondering it. He was. He wrote in his notebook, as he often does on the porch. I wagged my tail for a moment, then slept.

* * *

Chapter 5

The day that I found a 'possum in the yard

I should not have expected a simple discussion about bragging to change his view overnight, though I wanted it to. I knew that many humans were preoccupied with ideas about superiority, but I didn't realize how much those ideas affect their lives. Not just the obvious ways, not just the damage done by those people with an obvious, unhealthy desire for status and adulation, but also the subtle ways that affect intelligent and sensitive people like Leo. It is surprising how, in one moment, they pity someone who they've diagnosed as having low self-esteem, and in the next

The View from the Porch

moment, they're demanding that their own esteem be nurtured, without even realizing it.

It was only a few days after our conversation about Nick, that Leo was complaining about someone else who he believed had low self-esteem. He was so distracted by it that he didn't even notice that a 'possum had wondered into the yard and died of fright at the mere sound of my awesome bark. By the time I got Leo to take me back out to the yard to show him what I had done, the possum had somehow vanished. He looked at the tracks in the snow for a moment, but was not the least bit amazed, and instead, started telling me about his coworker, Jason, who had been causing frustration in meetings.

As we continued through the yard, past the thicket where the 'possum had died, and toward the park trail, Leo said: "Jack, your suggestions have been rolling around in my head and they seem to make sense, but ego is ego. I wonder if you're over-thinking things a bit. When someone is saying or doing something to boost his own ego, you can tell. And I think it's not always as harmless as you were suggesting. Ego-driven people can really create problems in a lot of situations.

"There is a guy at work, Jason, who is so obnoxious. We have these monthly staff meetings. I just recently began attending them. They asked me to start going, back when they first started talking about opening a new store. Anyway, when Jason gets started on an idea, he acts like he is the only one who ever had an idea. When we start discussing it, if someone disagrees with him, he gets really intense and animated and he gets in this mode where he is just ready to pick apart any suggestion that conflicts with his. It's like he can't even consider the possibility that someone else might be right."

Is he right?

"That's not the point. The point is that you have to be open to other people's ideas."

Even if they're wrong?

"They're not wrong. I mean they could be wrong, I guess, but he doesn't even give the idea a chance. He shoots it down because it's not his idea. It has nothing to do with wrong or right."

How does he shoot 'em down?

"He just finds some little nitpicky thing that he uses to show that the idea isn't good."

He invents flaws in their ideas?

The View from the Porch

"I don't know if I'd say that he *invents* flaws...I mean, every plan has pros and cons, but I would say that he focuses on the cons, just to show that his idea is better."

Was anyone else aware of these flaws in the plans?

"Probably, but they're minor flaws—"

Does anyone else initiate discussions about flaws in your company's plans?

"Sure, but he seems to have a knack for it. Especially, when—"

They're someone else's plans...I know, you've said that. So does anyone look for flaws in his plans?

"Yeah, I think we all do. We're tired of him imposing his will."

You attack his plans because you're tired of him?

Leo stopped and took a deep breath as we reached the trailhead in the park. He was getting frustrated. That usually means he's about to figure something out, but he persisted with the same argument as we entered the forest.

"I think maybe I am not explaining it right. The guy is an egomaniac. Why can't other people be right too?"

The trail curved to the bank of an icy stream. We stopped there to watch and listen. We had seen a mink diving from that bank months before. Since then, Leo always stopped to check for it.

I suppose Leo, that when a group of 5 people are sitting around trying to solve a problem, each one has 20% of the solution.

He said nothing. He zipped his coat to the top and pulled his hat down further over his ears. The sun was falling fast and the temperature with it. We started walking again.

"Well...no. Each person doesn't necessarily have 20% of the solution. Maybe someone has a better idea than someone else. But you still should have the respect for other people to hear them out...and find out what they do have to contribute. They may have 20%, or 40% or 80 or 100% of the solution!"

When they give their idea, how will you know if it's the solution? Will you test it?

"I guess in some situations you can test it, but in others..."

In others?

"In others you have to...talk it out. But you talk it out respectfully, giving everyone a chance to be heard...without your ego interfering with the process."

How can you tell it's his ego?

The View from the Porch

"What else would it be?"

That's a good question. What else could it be?

"Exactly."

No, really. Tell me something else it might be. Something else that you thought about, then ruled out.

"Uh...he...maybe..."

Your first thought was ego. And you stopped there.

"OK, yeah, I stopped there. You don't know the type of person he is. He can't take criticism."

What do you mean by taking the criticism?

"Well...thoughtfully considering someone else's point."

You mean taking the time to make other people feel special about their ideas? Like a good humble person would do? Like you would do?

"Yeah, what's wrong with that?"

Maybe he thinks he should be focused on the ideas, instead of on the self-esteem of his co-workers. Perhaps you're right. Perhaps he should be more sensitive to your esteem.

"It isn't about my esteem. Why does he have to be like a damned lawyer? It just makes everyone so defensive."

Yeah, I can tell.

Anyway, I thought you liked lawyers. You're always watching them on TV.

"Yeah, but lawyers argue for a living. I can respect them more than I can respect people who do it just to beat people down."

I think there is something significant in your appreciation of lawyers— something that you could apply here. See, a long time ago some of the smarter humans realized that if you really wanted to find the truth in a court of law, the best way to do it was to have people argue for both sides. And that each arguer had to try their best to win the argument. They believed that the truth would be the argument that is left standing.

"We weren't in a court room. We were in a staff meeting at a landscaping company."

Well, I guess that in staff meetings hyper-sensitive egos are more important than the truth.

Leo scoffed at my sarcasm, but we both knew where he stood on this matter. Truth is more important than ego, even in a staff meeting. He walked quietly for a while. He still wanted Jason to be guilty, but reasonable doubt was setting in. We reached a trail intersection and took the turn back toward the house.

The View from the Porch

Jason sets his idea out there in the world to be tested. He puts it out forcefully. A lot of people put their ideas out there gently, like you'd have him do, under the guise of diplomacy, and courtesy, when really it's about protecting their ego. Doesn't a person who stands firmly behind his argument stand to lose more when it is proven wrong?

"Yeah, but you could also say that he argues so forcefully because he's protecting his ego, an ego that couldn't stand it if he were shown to be wrong."

You could say that... and it sounds like that's what you are going to say. But you could say something else. Because he might be motivated by something else. You could say whatever you want though. Especially if you are not interested in looking past the same old argument you use to help you justify your own defense mechanisms. You humans, living in your self-esteem world have concocted this whole elaborate system of diagnosing low self-esteem, so you can feel like the educated humble one. If you had esteem, would you really care about how forceful he is? Wouldn't your focus be on the quality of his ideas?

"You really think I'm the one with self-esteem problems?"

I didn't know if it was a rhetorical question, so I didn't respond.

"Maybe I am a little too quick to call people on their self-esteem problems. But I really think that a lot of people suffer from it. And you can see it everywhere. Maybe I didn't really have a lot of evidence that Jason was really behaving that way just to boost his ego, but I've dealt with enough people to know what it looks like when a person is insecure."

We arrived back at the house. I got a drink while Leo put on some tea. I plopped down by the fireplace, hoping he would start a fire. He did. I was done talking for the night. Leo needed to think about this conversation for a while. His opinions about Jason sprung from a wound shared with co-workers. Other people were hurt by Jason's approach to meetings. Leo's response came, not only from his ego, but from empathy for his friends. There was some kindness in it, but if he really wanted to help his friends, he wouldn't reinforce their need to have their egos stroked. He could show them that when the desire to have your contribution recognized is greater than your desire for the truth, you probably won't contribute much. People who are working toward the truth see this. People who are working toward winning arguments do not.

* * *

Chapter 6

The day that Leo started some vegetables on the windowsill

After our discussion about Jason, Leo wanted to talk more, but he wasn't ready. I ignored a few attempts at conversation, when I sensed that it would end up the same as previous ones, with Leo trying to deny the possibility that his own esteem might be involved in the frustrations of his life. I had said enough. Though his insecurities were indeed small and few, he needed to admit them. And he had to come to it on his own time.

The View from the Porch

That discussion began on the day he put the seeds in the tray on the window sill. I watched as he spread out seed envelopes and scooped soil into trays. I wagged my tail, knowing that plants would soon sprout in those trays. And soon it would be warm enough to put them outside. And then we would be spending more time out in the fresh air. He would rest in the hammock, or stand in the garden waiting for his tomatoes and peppers to be ready for the salsa. When he works on his vegetables, whether he is placing the tiny seeds into the pots, or tying up the stalks to keep his giant tomatoes from collapsing to the dirt, he always seems at his best. He seems more peaceful when he's working toward producing something real, like those fat tomatoes that he slices into pieces and eats like a steak.

As he pressed the seeds into their little squares of soil I could see that the busy thoughts that kept him from admitting his insecurities were quieting. I could see that he was about to say something good. It didn't take him long. He bravely waded into it one evening while we watched a gentle rain melt the last piles of dirty snow into the grass.

"Jack, I've decided, for the sake of moving forward with our conversation, I would search out any bit of esteem issues that might be hiding in the nooks and crannies of my brain. It isn't really that I thought they didn't exist. I just don't think they have a very strong influence on my behavior. Especially when compared with the insecure people that I deal with daily. That's what I was trying to talk to you about, but you don't...ah, anyway. I guess it's just because you want to hear me bring up some of my own issues first. Fine.

I guess there are some things that sometimes make me feel...a little uncomfortable."

I wagged. And turned to look over my shoulder at him.

"I kind of wish I had finished college, for example."

I stood up, walked in a circle, then plopped down facing him, so he knew I was listening.

"And I guess that when people start talking about college it gives me an uncomfortable feeling. It isn't that I feel dumb though. I know I'm an intelligent guy. It just seems like people talk to you a little differently if you tell them you have a degree. There are a few kids at work, like Jason, who are fresh out of college. They don't have a lick of experience in anything real, but the world seems all laid out for them. I'm as smart as they are, plus I have some experience. But here I am. My life isn't bad. But it sometimes seems like the people who are educated enough to engage me in an interesting conversation aren't interested in talking to

The View from the Porch

me if they find out I don't have a degree. Or maybe they just assume that I don't have a degree because I do physical labor.

"Anyway, that's something. That's something about me that I wish was different. Something about me that I am not too proud of."

I waited for more.

"Um. What else? Let's see. Um, sometimes... if Liz mentions her ex-husband, or an ex-boyfriend, who all went to college and have successful careers, I get a little twisted. If we see one of them out somewhere, I find myself in a negative train of thought. Maybe I focus on some derogatory thing she once said about them, so I can think about that flaw instead of thinking about the fact that I can't afford to take her to all of the places they used to go together. I guess I do worry that she might secretly wish she could still go out and do all of those fancy things. Go to the Caribbean every year. Go to nice restaurants every weekend. And those guys now have nice houses in Knollwood, and I live in this tiny thing.

"She and I have fun. I like our life. But I guess I worry sometimes that she doesn't like it as much as I do. And I guess that qualifies as insecurity."

He still had my attention, but he seemed to want to be done. I didn't think he was, so I waited.

"Yeah, this little house needs some work. Perhaps I'm embarrassed by it sometimes. I can't afford to get a bigger one. I mean, the house is fine. Everything is solid, but… it's pretty small, there's not a lot of extra room. There's no office. No master bath with a garden tub. Maybe if I had some money— maybe if I took that job I could move into something a little better. Or at least fix this one up. I've wanted to get new siding. Maybe a new front door. It would really make this place look a lot better. But I guess, if I don't really need all that stuff, then my concern about it…well, maybe I just wish I had a better house.

"I think that's about it though."

I waited still. I didn't want to let him off the hook until he thought of everything.

"Um, I guess sometimes I think about the glory days of football. I was tougher then. And people knew I was tough. I can admit that I liked that. I can admit that I like when I see Jay or Pete and they bring up a play in some playoff game where I smashed someone. My ego gets a little boost from that."

The View from the Porch

It's OK to get a little boost from that.

"It is?"

Yeah. You might want to think about aiming for a state of mind in which such things aren't necessary. Perhaps you will never achieve a state of mind in which you don't enjoy a compliment, but you can find a path that doesn't require those compliments... those words that other people use to describe you. It feels good to hear nice words about your behavior. But if you change your behavior just to hear them, it's not good.

"Do you think I change my behavior for them?"

Not for compliments, per se. But perhaps for identity, for that idea you have about who you are. You want to be identified as someone who provides for his girlfriend. Someone who is tough and athletic. Someone who is intelligent.

You altered your path when you criticized your coworker for thinking he is always right. His ideas are good. And if you weren't so upset about his forcefulness, which stands in the way of people identifying you as intelligent, you would see that he has quality ideas.

He sat silently with this for a while. There was an objection on the tip of his tongue, but he said nothing. Either he couldn't find the words for it or he was starting to realize that if he gave my ideas some time, he'd discover the truth in them.

He gathered his tea cup and his notebook. "Come on Pup," he said, as he opened the sliding door into the house. I walked to the bedroom as he put his cup in the sink and began preparing his lunch for the next day.

It was one of our most important conversations. Not because Leo's self-esteem was in desperate need of repair. He didn't have what most humans would call low self-esteem. Up to that point his few insecurities had not kept him from creating and enjoying a pretty good life. His feelings about his identity were mostly positive, but, like most people, he thought that he had things figured out just because he liked his answer to the question "How am I thought of?" As long as he believed it was an important question, he was bound to slip up. The health of his esteem is not determined by his answer to that question. It is determined by how much he needs to ask it. Almost every human struggles with that. Even the rich ones with college degrees.

* * *

Chapter 7

The day that we watched
bees on the wildflowers

Throughout our conversations, Leo and I were pretty loose with our terminology. Entire books have been written attempting to define words like ego, identity, esteem and self. And yet we used them often, without a lot of discussion of what we meant. I guess we just always understood what the other intended. And in this book we have resisted the urge to define those things thus far, choosing to let the readers use their own impressions of those words to make meaning out of all of this. But there was one conversation

The View from the Porch

about separating certain terms and I think it's necessary to include it.

We were walking on the trail with the wooden bridge over the ravine. I didn't care for that bridge because my toes slipped into the cracks. But Leo liked it, especially in the spring when the wildflowers along the ravine were in bloom. He stopped and crouched to a tiny white flower with a bee on it. This was not the kind of bee we see in the summer. These bees have burrows in the sandy soil by the picnic area, close to the woods so they can pollinate the spring woodland wildflowers. Dozens of them fly low around their burrows. Normally Leo doesn't let me chase wild things, but when we reached their burrows he sat on the picnic table and laughed as I tried to catch them. I didn't have any luck. When I gave up, he called me over to sit at his feet for a while. He breathed deeply and smelled the air. He looked calm. I could tell he wanted to talk.

He said, "Today I was talking to a new guy at work who likes to write. We were talking about authors and writing. I told him that I enjoy writing and mentioned that my writing needs some work. He said, 'Oh I'm sure you're great.' Which reminded me of something you said a while ago: that if someone feels inferior, other people intervene to make him feel superior. But it also made me think about the difference between confidence and self-esteem. Does it mean that I have low self-esteem just because I think my writing needs some work?"

Self-esteem has nothing to do with it. Confidence is something else. I think you understand the difference.

"I do?"

Yeah. What is it?

"Um...I guess that confidence is what you think you can do, and self-esteem is...more like...what you think you are."

Yeah. If you get in the ring with the heavyweight champion of the world, you're aware of the fact that you don't have the training and experience to defeat him. This doesn't mean that you don't have self-esteem. It means you are realistic. Perhaps there is some young boxer somewhere, who could train hard and become the world champ, but if he thinks, "I could never become the champ", then for him, maybe it is about self-esteem. You? You aren't training. You are healthy and fit, but you don't have a young body anymore. So you admit, it would be a long shot at best. That's logical. That's a lack of confidence, not a lack of esteem. We're getting into too much definition here, but I guess it is important to understand that difference.

* * *

Chapter 8

The day that Leo saw a warbler visit the bird bath

Changing someone's mind about a habit is hard enough. If he is convinced that the habit is actually one of his strengths, it is even harder. Leo had the habit of overcoming problems. Humans often confuse *overcoming* with *solving*. In most cases, they don't even think about the difference. Apparently, Leo hadn't. It caused a fight between he and Liz.

One afternoon, he returned home in a crummy mood. We only went for a short walk, then I had to whine to get

The View from the Porch

him to sit on the back porch with me. When he finally joined me, an unfamiliar bird splashing in the bird bath caught his eye. He looked it up in the book he kept in the drawer by his chair, but not even a new bird could lift his spirits. I could see that he needed consolation. I went to the edge of his chair to shake. I put my paw on his knee and he rubbed my head. He lost concentration and stared out the window, so I put my head on his knee.

"Thanks Pup. Yeah, I'm sorry we didn't go for a longer walk today. Liz and I had an argument."

My head was still on his knee, so he rubbed it as he told me about the disagreement.

"I know she just wants me to listen sometimes. I know that I don't have to be the solution to her problems. I just need to let her talk it out sometimes... but she was complaining—"

He shrugged his shoulders and tried to convince himself that the argument was too silly to talk about, but he talked anyway.

"I was just giving her a suggestion and I guess she didn't think she needed it. She was complaining about the cup-holder in her car. When you pull out the cup-holder to put in a cup, it hangs down and you can't see the heater controls. I was just telling her that there are only a few positions on the heater dial and it's easy enough to just memorize them and reach under there and turn the knob below the cup. She got mad. She said I always do that. She said that it wasn't that she couldn't figure out a solution. I don't know why she had to be so defensive. I... she..."

I pulled away from his hand.

"You are going to tell me that she was right, aren't you?"

Was she right?

"Was she right about what?"

The cup-holder, for starters.

"Well, yeah it's in the way, but it isn't impossible to overcome the problem."

And you're the one who knows how to overcome it. Good job.

"Alright. Judging by your sarcasm you're about to tell me I need to think about this differently...It isn't about the cup-holder...Umm. No, wait...it has something to do with identity."

Are you mocking my advice?

The View from the Porch

"Why does it have to be self-esteem problems that make me want to overcome a problem? There are a lot of people out there who would rather just complain about a situation. Instead of fixing it."

Did you fix it?

"Yeah!"

The cup-holder is not in the way anymore?

"It's in the way still, but it's not a problem."

And that's why Liz brought it up? Because she couldn't find a way around the problem?

"She's an intelligent person. I'm sure she could find a way around it. I'm sure she could work the heater, even with the cup-holder down."

So she wasn't stumped with this obstacle, she was just commenting on it?

"I guess."

How much did she pay for that car?

"I don't know, maybe twenty thousand."

And the people who designed it have engineering degrees and make a lot of money?

"Probably."

You trust these people to create something that will move you down the highway safely at seventy miles an hour, but you think asking these geniuses for a well-placed cup-holder is unreasonable?

"Yeah, I imagine they could come up with something better."

They won't though. Unless every person who sits down in the driver seat to test-drive a car looks down at the cup-holder and the heater controls and says, "This is not quality, and I won't buy this," the lazy engineer who designed the car will make next year's model just as bad.

And maybe Liz was just venting. Perhaps she has no intention of writing the manufacturer, or switching brands the next time she buys, or doing anything else that could bring quality to the world of car cup-holders. But don't confuse overcoming with fixing. When you overcome a problem, you are not adding quality to the world like you do when you fix a problem. Have you ever really thought about the difference? What you wanted Liz to do is provide a temporary solution for herself. What she was talking about was a permanent solution for future car owners. She was talking about fixing the problem. People often let overcoming *take the place of* fixing. *Why do you think people do that?*

The View from the Porch

He shrugged, then sat quietly for moment, before saying, "Maybe we're just lazy."

Sometimes. And sometimes overcoming some minor thing makes more sense and takes less time then going through the trouble of fixing it. But other times overcoming is about you and what you can do. Sometimes it's about something you can take pride in. How many low-quality products and situations are perpetuated by the pride we take in overcoming an obstacle?

"A lot, I suppose."

He sipped his tea.

"So this is about my desire to be identified as someone who can overcome obstacles?"

I nodded and plopped down on the rug.

"Is this how it will always go? If I share the frustrations in my life, you'll respond with some way that my own ego is causing the frustration? This isn't exactly boosting my self-esteem."

I don't want to boost your self-esteem.

"Then what are you trying to do?"

I'm trying to show you that self-esteem is not real.

"Not real! It's real, Pup. I see it all the time. There are so many people with self-esteem issues that are messing up their lives! And messing up other people's lives. It's real, Pup."

Of course there are some people who have problems because they think poorly of themselves. But the same old conversations about self-esteem aren't helping anyone. Because people aren't even really thinking about what it means to have self-esteem.

A person supposedly has low self-esteem if the words he uses in his thoughts to describe himself are not positive words. So he believes that he could be happy if he could just believe that positive words are the real description. It never works though. Because the problem is not the words you use – the problem is that you believe the description is a real thing.

"But there is a real description of me, Pup. I'm a boyfriend, a laborer, a homeowner."

As far as descriptions go, those descriptions are true. Does that mean it is real? Are those descriptions real things?

"Well, I'm really Liz's boyfriend. And there's no way to trick my mind into thinking that I'm not Liz's boyfriend, that I don't have a job as a laborer, that I don't own this little house. And if there are derogatory words that describe me, I can't trick my mind into thinking there aren't."

The View from the Porch

You don't need to trick your mind into thinking that the descriptions aren't true. You just have to look at how much truth they can actually hold. That is what I mean when I say they aren't real. How much of the truth about your relationship with Liz does the word 'boyfriend' hold? The word boyfriend is not the cause of the good feelings you have when you are with Liz, it's just one insignificant result. The least important aspect of your boyfriendness, is its description. There are so many real experiences that you have because of Liz, and every one of them, every sight, smell, touch, taste and feeling that is activated by her presence in your life is more real, more tangible, than descriptions. Am I right? Do you need to trick yourself into believing that? Yes, every situation in your life could be described, but when will that description be the most important element of the situation? How does the description of your job compare to other realities of your job? The money it gives you to eat and live? The exercise it gives you to stay strong? The awe you experience when you see a hawk? Isn't it obvious that these things are more tangible and real, and therefore more important than a description. All you have to do is point your mind at the very real truth that only a fool invests his energy in descriptions.

And, of course, the description people spend the most energy on, is the description of themselves. They carry around this set of words, this description, and they call it the self. And they put so much energy into liking it. But liking yourself won't solve anything. If that is your goal in life, how can you hope to enjoy anything real, anything more tangible than words? Because when you like your description all you're liking is words, and you can't feel words.

Leo stood from his chair, walked to the kitchen to warm up his tea, then returned to the porch, where he stood and watched the birds.

"I guess you can't feel words," he said, as he finally sat back down. "You can just think them, but...but if there are good words that describe me or something that I did, and I think about them, then I can really feel pride."

Pride. That's it. That's the whole reason humans have traded in their peace and joy... for a description... because once in a while when you like the description of you, and you can get other people to like it too, you can feel pride. But what if, instead of feeling proud, you felt comfortable? What if, instead of feeling proud, you felt wonder and amazement at the beauty of nature? What if you felt warmth? What if you tasted and touched and listened and smelled the world? What if the circumstances of your life were more important than the description of it? What if you let your mind experience the real things that you can feel and touch and hear and see...instead of forcing it to experience all those meaningless descriptions that occasionally let you feel pride? And you'll never

The View from the Porch

get enough pride anyway. Find me a person who isn't looking for more pride. It's like finding a person who isn't looking for more money. And you don't need it. Do you really think there is not enough to enjoy in this world without leaning on pride to help you enjoy it? What about holding hands? What about flowers? What about fresh fruit? What about laughter? What about music? Will you run out of things to enjoy in this life? How much more of these things could you enjoy if you spent less energy on the possibility of getting enough pride.

He didn't answer me, but I knew it hit him hard. He stared out into the yard considering other things on the list I had started. Birds, art, cooking, gardening, discovery, curiosity, revelation, books, women, skin, embraces and on and on. He was, at that moment, feeling the joy of all of those things.

If you could give up pride, Leo... if you could trade it in for increased awareness of all of those things, wouldn't you? Shouldn't you?

He nodded his head slowly without looking down at me. He sat silently and drank three more cups of tea before finally going to bed.

* * *

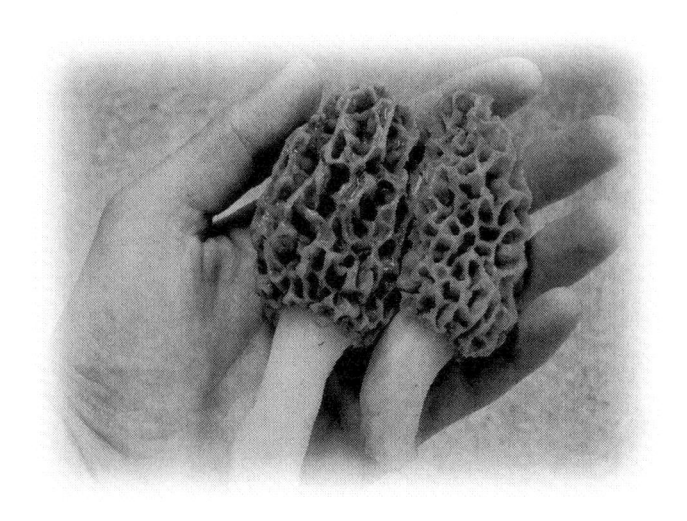

Chapter 9

The day Leo found the mushrooms in the woods, and the weeks that followed

Our hikes in the spring have their own kind of energy. It is not just the new life coming up all around us. Leo observes the forest in a completely different way. He stops every so often, crouches low like he might hug me, but instead reaches out with his walking stick to part the umbrella-shaped leaves. Occasionally, he'll find his treasure: morels. When he spots them he becomes a wild thing. He is like the hawk he watched that winter day, focused, intense and aware. On the day he found the first mushrooms of the year,

The View from the Porch

that intensity and awareness seemed to spill over into our conversation on the porch and lasted for the next few weeks.

Instead of resisting what I had told him, like he had after every other conversation, he had apparently absorbed what I shared in our last talk and started seeing examples of it everywhere. He was very quiet for two weeks, then suddenly, on the day he found the mushrooms in the woods, it was as if days of pent up observations came pouring out of him. Our evenings on the porch turned from peaceful meditations to energetic rants.

It began as he stood at the kitchen sink cleaning mushrooms. I squeezed into the space in front of his shins on the kitchen's only rug.

"I've been watching people at work and around town and I can't stop seeing examples of what you've been saying," he said. "And I could see it in this controversy on the news about this comedian that offended a bunch of people at one of his shows."

"All kinds of groups are calling for a boycott and want a public apology. The guy shouldn't have used those words in hostility, but it makes me wonder about what we are teaching young people. Is it more important that kids are taught not to use offensive words, or that they understand that words only have the power that we give them? Aren't we teaching them to invest in a description?"

He paused for a moment, like he was waiting for an answer, but then he continued.

"I took my nephew Luke fishing last summer. He had been having some behavioral problems—fighting at school. He thought that punching a classmate in the nose was justified because the kid disrespected him. I tried to tell him that the disrespectful words didn't actually take anything from him. There was no actual loss. Just a bunch of consonants and vowels out of some kid's mouth. It's already difficult enough to convince a 15-year old of this. It is even more difficult when some story hits the news about some inappropriate, politically incorrect thing that somebody said. A drunken actor blaming Jews for his arrest. A comic strip that offends half the world by mocking their deity. And every time this happens, the media succeeds in making teenagers and other insecure people feel wounded. How can I get my nephew to stop fighting over words when the media keeps telling him that words are such a threat?"

I didn't respond to any of it. He was heading in the right direction, but I felt a little bad for him. Leo will probably be alone in that belief for a while. Other humans will catch on,

The View from the Porch

but for now, their messages are often contradictory on this point. Especially from the people who think they have self-esteem all figured out. They are the ones who are so invested in helping everyone's esteem, yet they are the ones who let words have so much power. Words don't have power unless you give it to them. I wanted to explain all of this to him, but I decided to just let him work on his own for a while and let the momentum of his new intensity take him toward the right decision about the house.

He finished cleaning the mushrooms. He left most of them soaking in a pot, except for a small handful that he tossed in batter and fried. "I don't think you'd like 'em," he said, as he piled the mushrooms on his plate beside a sandwich. "And I gotta share these with Liz." He handed me a rawhide as he sat down with his meal. It was a good night.

As the mushroom season progressed, his intensity continued. Our walks, our dinners, and our back porch conversations were filled with philosophical observations. Everywhere he looked he saw humans wasting energy, trying to create and maintain a positive description for themselves.

"I've been seeing how we could get more out of everyday conversations if people could get this esteem thing figured out," he said one evening. "This guy came into work today to ask about moving his vegetables outside. But then he started talking about how he likes nature and how I must like nature and how cool my job is. He starts going on and on. Next thing I know he's telling me about his vacation in California and a whale watching trip that he went on. He was really starting to get on my nerves because I had a lot of work to do and he wasn't really talking about work-related stuff anymore. Then the guy stops, looks me right in the face and says, 'Um, is any of this interesting to you?' It was strange. He wasn't embarrassed. He wasn't being sarcastic. He seemed completely OK with the possibility that I might not care what he was saying. He thought he had something interesting to say, then realized it might not be interesting to me. For some reason it fascinated me that he had the ability to do that."

What did you say to him?

"Well. I didn't know what to say. He caught me off guard. 'Oh no, that's really cool. I bet whale watching is great.' Which, of course, made him start up again.

"I keep thinking, 'Why didn't I just tell him I needed to go back to work?' Maybe I thought I was doing him a favor. He was probably lonely. But he did ask me if I was interested in the conversation. I couldn't admit that I really wasn't."

The View from the Porch

I got up and repositioned myself, plopping down to face him. I was curious where he was going with this one.

"I think that I really didn't treat this guy respectfully. On the surface, it seems that I did. In fact it might seem compassionate. After all I might have been the only person he talked to all day. And maybe he just needed someone to listen to him for a while.

"But when I think about it now I realize that he was probably stronger than I thought. I assumed that if I said, 'Actually, I'm pretty busy' that he would have been offended. Or he would have suddenly felt foolish when he realized that I had really been trying to get away from him.

"Would I have been offended if I were him? I don't think I would have."

"I am an introspective person. A person who analyzes my own strategies and behaviors and makes changes when necessary. I can handle criticism. I can handle the truth, even when it's a hard truth about me or something I've done. In fact, it's not just that I can handle the hard truth— I really desire the truth. I would feel embarrassed if I found out someone was keeping it from me. Especially truths about my own mistakes."

"Did this man today desire the truth? He probably did. I didn't give it to him. I treated him as if he was not strong enough to handle it. I treated him as if he was not as strong as me. How arrogant? How righteous of me to claim this strength as my own, and not give another person the chance to reveal his strength. Perhaps he would have been offended. Perhaps his ego would have suffered. Perhaps he would have even complained to my boss that I was rude. But maybe he goes around talking to people that way all day. Perhaps my honesty could have been the truth that would have led him to an evaluation of his conversation skills. What if I had simply said, 'This conversation isn't about work anymore, and I have work to do, so unless you have more questions about plants I need to leave you now'?

"The more I thought about it today, the more I thought that there must be a world of people out there who really want direct honest conversations. People like me. But do we get those conversations? No. We get superficial niceties from people who think they are doing something good for us.

"Perhaps it would have been a problem if I were more direct with this guy today. Even though he was aware enough to ask if I was interested in the conversation, he might have felt embarrassed. He might have felt criticized.

The View from the Porch

Criticism, even constructive criticism, almost always causes problems. But why? Because some people abuse the tool of criticism, and use it to make people feel low? Ever since pop-psychology got hold of those abusive critics and declared that they were only criticizing because they feel insecure, it has wrecked the tool of criticism. Now, when we are criticized, we can dismiss it as a symptom of the critic's low self-esteem. And when we have an opportunity to offer truthful, constructive criticism to someone, we withhold it—as an act of self-righteous humility or in an effort to protect their fragile esteem, to maintain their notion of their identity. If we looked at criticism as a potentially valuable outside perspective— if we could consider it without regard to our ego or the ego of the critic, what truths would we discover?

"What would it be like if constructive criticism were the custom? I'm not talking about verbal abuse. I'm not talking about when people belittle others to build up their own identity. But what if we all addressed behaviors honestly and openly? What if we believed that when someone was commenting on our behavior there was no offense to our person, no identity to suffer?"

He took the long deep breath he needed after all of that talking. He stopped and finished the last of his tea. He was done talking for the night and I was glad, not because I was uninterested, but because I was worried that this project, this new approach, would wear him out. It nearly did. Even in the simplest human interactions Leo found evidence that the human desire to create a positive description caused problems. It was a frustrating time for Leo, and our talks during that time were characterized by that frustration. Those conversations became redundant, which is why I decided that they did not need to be shared verbatim like our earlier discussions.

Each story seemed to start as if it were a new topic, but by the end it would become clear that Leo was continually frustrated by different variations of the same human flaw. He talked about how the internet lets people create a profile and how the creation of this profile reinforces a person's habit of thinking about their own description. He saw countless examples of human dependence on praise, and just as many examples of how that dependence is reinforced by family, friends and coworkers. He talked about how a mob mentality has been fundamental to the worst human atrocities and how that mentality depends on the desire to be identified in a certain way. He talked about the purest moments of human experience, when there are no thoughts of one's identity, and about how tragic it is that humans forget the power of those moments. Perhaps a patient dog, (or his student) will some

The View from the Porch

day catalog all of Leo's observations in a text book of canine wisdom. Until then, in this abridged version, it is enough to say that all his observations were different versions of the same few related ideas: that most people, including those who think they understand self-esteem, are unaware of how much time and energy they invest in creating and maintaining a positive descriptions for themselves, how much they foster this same behavior in others, and how much peace it costs everyone.

Finally, one evening in May, I was able to pull him away from his vigilant search. Our walk that night began with the same intensity that had been pushing him for weeks. He searched for mushrooms again, but if there were any left they were buried below the mayapples, trout lilies and trillium. Walking home with an empty mushroom bag, he turned his appreciation toward the wildflowers, stopping twice to inspect the blossoms of anemones.

When we returned he made tea and we went to the porch. He barely had his first sip, when he began, "I was at the grocery store today—" but I cut him off before he could get into it. I got up and nuzzled against his leg so he would rub my ears. I'm not sure if that was for his benefit or mine. I didn't really want another story. And I think he didn't really want to tell me one. It was time for him to slow down and I didn't even have to tell him. "OK. OK, Pup," he said.

Some wise human once wrote about a cat, "My cat's greatest gift to me is that she wants from me what I should want from myself, that I sit and be still." Even though it was said about a cat, I admit that it's true. It's true about dogs sometimes, too.

* * *

Chapter 10

The day that Leo found the praying mantis eggs

The deadline for Leo's decision about the new job neared and I still didn't know if we'd be moving away from our cozy home at the edge of the park.

Leo's back porch rants had quieted. He seemed to have much on his mind, but he wasn't sharing it. I could see it approaching though. There was one thing I knew we had left to discuss, and I could tell he was thinking about it. I could see it in the way he breathed while we sat on the porch. I could see it in how he watched wildlife in the park.

The View from the Porch

As we walked along the fencerow between the forest and the field, he found a praying mantis egg case on an autumn olive bush. He stooped low to look at it, and said, "It makes me wonder about the park's management plan for autumn olive. It isn't native, and it'll crowd out other plants and reduce diversity. All of the old fields in the park that aren't actively managed and burned are full of it. The staff plans to try to eradicate it, but what will that mean to the mantis? Not much, maybe, because the mantis can lay her eggs on any stem that will last the winter. I've seen them on goldenrod. In fact, it probably isn't even a native mantis. But what about all the birds that are now accustomed to eating the olive fruits in the fall, or even nesting in it in the spring? What will they do instead?"

I had no answer for him. But I sensed that he was ready to ask another big question. A question that might allow us to complete our conversation. We walked quietly back to the house.

After dinner that evening, he made tea and we went to the back porch.

"Pup, tell me something. I like all this stuff you've been saying, but I keep coming back to something. It seems like if everyone really did accept all of this that you've been saying it might leave some pretty big holes. The idea of our unique identity...the idea of feeling good about ourselves, it's been our rudder. Many people who accomplished great things did so because they were trying to build a life they could be proud of. If you take that away, won't you just have people fulfilling their own selfish needs?

I don't think it would be such a disaster.

"Well, if someone is just focused on their own comfort and peace, instead of on what the world thinks of him, that might be fine, depending on what brings him comfort. But what if...what if there's some guy who is a real jerk. A bully. Or maybe he's a thief or scammer. Doesn't matter— maybe he's just rude to waiters or something like that. Now let's say that he decides he wants to turn his life around. He's trying to turn his life around because he wants to be a better person. He may not use the words you use, but his desire to be a better person is really a desire to have a better description, a better identity. Now should we really try to convince him that there is no such thing?"

Maybe.

"Why would he ever change his behavior? Doesn't he need identity in order to answer the question: Am I a good person? Don't we want him to ask that question?"

The View from the Porch

The question we really want him to ask, and answer, is: Is this behavior going to bring me peace and comfort?

"But what if one man's peace and comfort leads to the pain and misery of the people around him? Don't we just open the door for every man to do what he wants, despite the effect on the rest of us?"

I don't think so. By opening this door, we let everyone find out that we all want the same thing.

"Well that sounds just lovely, but we don't all want the same thing. Our desires are immeasurably diverse and complicated."

Are they?

"Of course they are."

I waited silently.

"Our interests, our hobbies, our values, our religions, lead us to a million desires at least."

There may be a million desires. And it's nice to have a variety of desirable things in the world. But if everyone is focused on the diversity of desires, it's no wonder that they can't seem to fulfill the only desires that really count.

"Which desires are those?"

I think you know.

"I…"

I think you see that you can behave in a way that sets you apart and gives you the identity, the description you think you need. Or…

"Or?"

Or you can fulfill your true desires.

"Which are?"

I waited. He looked out across the yard. He breathed deeply. He sipped his tea. Then said, "To give and receive love."

I wagged my tail.

It's your strongest desire. And it's the same strongest desire that every one has. You know that no matter what identity you succeed in creating for yourself, no matter how unique and special you become, no matter how you might be described, you don't want to be the sole owner of the behaviors that elicit love: compassion, openness, kindness. If those behaviors were yours and yours alone, whom would you love?

The View from the Porch

He sipped his tea. He breathed deeply. He listened to each note of each song that was being sung by the birds in the yard.

"Could it be that simple? How could we fail to see something so simple?"

You wanted it to be complicated.

"Because the identity we think we need, the esteem we think we need, lies in those complications, in too many words about our strengths and weaknesses... in too many words about our differences, so we could...so we could create a unique identity."

He sipped his tea. He breathed deeply.

"Why do we want that so badly? It seems so foolish. So selfish."

It's really a pretty innocent mistake.

"How can it be? It just seems so obvious."

There is a loving intent behind it all. Humans know, even if they don't think about it this way, that when someone believes that you are good and unique, then you exist in their mind as more than just a fact, a body and a name. You exist there as a good feeling. I guess you'd say that you exist in their heart. And that is signifi-

cant. That is real. Because if you exist there as a good feeling, they might try to spend time with you and get that good feeling again. You want people to want to spend time with you. It's understandable that you seek out such a thing. Perhaps it's just your love of words that mucked it all up. You just have too many words, too many descriptions for how a person can be good, for how a person can be desirable. But you only really need a few. Then you need to have the patience and trust in your fellow humans to know that if you can master those few, you will be loved as much as you can handle. All those other descriptions you want to use for an identity, it's just a bunch of unnecessary salesmanship. The more contrived an identity, the more fragile your presence is in other people's minds and hearts. You can be present there with little or no effort.

"The way you are present in mine."

Think about the words you use in your mind to describe me. They're pretty simple aren't they?

He nodded.

But I'm there aren't I. In your mind, and in your heart?

He nodded again. He closed his eyes as he took a long slow breath, then opened them as he exhaled. He looked down at me and slapped his knee to ask me to step onto his lap. When I did he pulled me close and put his cheek against mine. I stepped down and we walked to the window to watch the birds.

"I think everything is going to be good for me Jack. But I don't know if people will give up their quest for a unique identity easily. It's going to be pretty hard."

People seem to find everything hard. But they'll get it. It starts with just realizing there is no law that demands that you have an opinion about yourself. There's no law that says you have to spend all this time working on something as intangible and irrelevant as an identity, even if everyone else seems to be wasting their time working on it. And when you succeed in shifting your focus from your identity toward more tangible and enjoyable things, then good things will start to grow in your lives. And when the good things start to grow, the weed that was your attempt at a unique identity will get pushed to the edge of the field and forgotten.

"Is that going to make us all alike?"

No. Diverse interests and skills will flower, effortlessly, and make everyone interesting and peaceful, like they always wanted to be.

We sat quietly for another hour before going to bed.

* * *

Chapter 11

***On the day that Leo planted
the vegetables in the garden***

When Leo returned from work the next day he loaded up the red wagon with some tools, jars of seed and six of the plants that he had been growing on the windowsill. I followed him out to the sunny spot behind the garage, where he began digging at the soil. I plopped down in the grass by the small white fence that surrounds the sunny spot. He worked until the sun turned the sky orange and purple out of over the park.

The View from the Porch

When we returned to the house he poured himself a glass of lemonade and called me to the porch.

"Well, Pup, I decided that I'm not going to take that new position," he said. "I enjoy what I do. And I enjoy this home and this yard. After I get those veggies going, I'll plant some native wildflowers along the fencerow. I think it will bring even more birds and other wildlife back here. I think it will make the view from the porch even better."

It was the right choice. It isn't that taking a promotion is wrong, but when Leo thought honestly about what makes him happy, he realized that taking the promotion wouldn't have given him that. It would have given him something, but he had stopped caring about that something.

"Yeah, we're staying. I told Liz I really like this little house. And this porch. This porch is a sacred gift, not because of how it looks from out there, but because of what I am able to see from it. I told her that we couldn't replace this view for ten times the price of this little house. She said, 'Of course.' She said that she has always wanted to share this view with me, but didn't want to seem pushy about moving in. So you won't mind another person around here all the time, will you?

"And I let my boss know that I was interested in maybe helping out with some gardening classes. She sounded willing, enthusiastic even, about letting me teach a few workshops. I think I would enjoy that. My schedule won't change much. I think I'll still have plenty of time to spend out here with you, Pup."

I got up and stepped my front legs onto his lap and looked him in the eye. I said nothing, but my message was clear to him. He didn't need to hear any more words to know how much I appreciated what he had done. For a human, it is a major feat to ignore the idea of identity and focus on tangible consequences. He hadn't realized how far he'd come, how many silly human habits he'd broken. I wagged my tail, but still said nothing. There was nothing left to say.

"You know Jack, you've really helped me. I've been thinking about how you live. And how wise you seem to be. I've been thinking about the words you would use to help me understand it all. But...well, it's been nice talking to you Jack, but we can be silent for a while. I don't need words to enjoy your company. I guess that's what you were trying to tell me from the beginning."

I wagged my tail, stepped down from his thigh and curled up by his feet as he drank his lemonade.

* * *

Made in the USA
Charleston, SC
15 September 2012